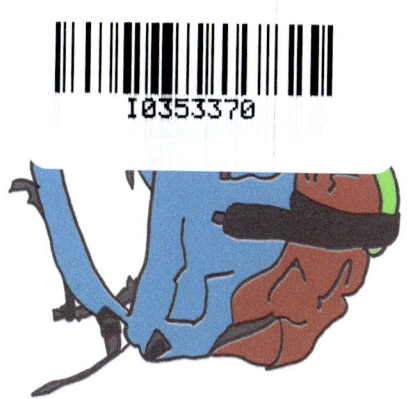

For all the rescue pups of the world. May your forever home be filled with love, laughs and loads of treats.

Copyright © 2022 Lisa Blake and Nadine Rebrovic

All rights reserved.

No part of this publication in print or in electronic format may be reproduced, stored in a retrieval system, or transmitted in any form or by any means, electronic, mechanical, photocopying, recording, or otherwise without the prior written permission of the publisher.

This is a work of fiction. Names, characters, organizations, places, events and incidents are either the products of the author's imagination or are used fictitiously. Any resemblance to actual persons, living or dead, or actual events is purely coincidental.

Cover Art by Nadine Rebrovic
Design by Hilary Stojak
Distribution by Bublish

Paperback: 978-1-64704-504-3
Hardcover: 978-1-64704-505-0

HOW TO LOVE YOUR RESCUE PUP

10 SIMPLE RULES
FOR TAKING THE VERY BEST CARE OF YOUR SPECIAL FURRY FRIEND

WRITTEN BY LISA BLAKE
ILLUSTRATED BY NADINE REBROVIC

There are
10 simple rules
for taking the very
best care of
your rescue pup.

First, trust.

Speak **calmly** and **softly**. Show your pup **patience** and **unconditional love**. Some dogs take extra time to trust their humans.

Don't give up on them.

Next, safety.

Use gentle hands and gentle voices. Make a space for them to call their own. Even if you aren't their first home, you are their forever home.

Then comes bonding.

10

Explore and **be wild** with your rescue pup. Have **fun** and **cherish** your time. The more adventures you have **together**, the **stronger your bond** grows.

Know that all dogs are beautiful.

Three-legged, one-eyed,
young and **clumsy**.

There's a
special home
for every pup.

 ## Listen very carefully.

A happy pooch has
soft, relaxed ears and eyes,
a wagging tail
and a big easy smile.

If they show their teeth or growl,
give them space.

 Be silly.

Come up with funny **nicknames** for your rescue pup, like Scrappy Wappy, Mr. Pickles or Sir Wiggle Bottom. Get on all fours, play **tug-of-war** and roll around together. Rescue doggies love all the **giggles** and **fun**.

Share your world.

Eat together, **play** together,
walk to the park together.
Let your pup **sleep** in your room.
Show them your **favorite** books, lovies,
trails and trees.

Feed them yummy foods.

Find out what your pup loves to eat. Maybe it's steak or chicken. Maybe your pup is a vegetarian.

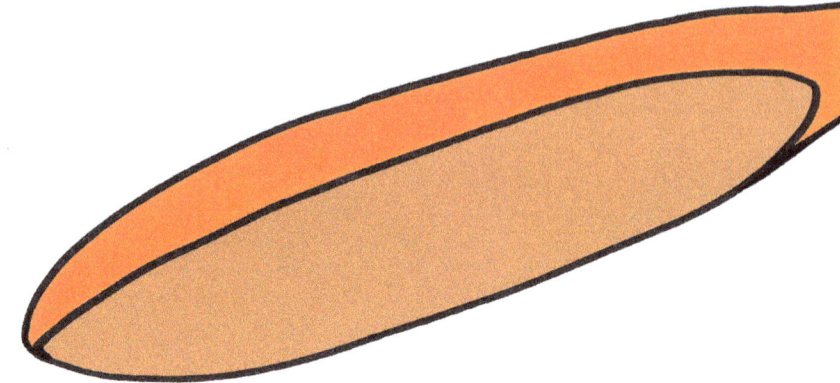

 Have fun together.

A rescue pup is never too old or shy to have fun. Play games, run through sprinklers, throw a Frisbee or just watch your favorite show together and snuggle.

Finally, the most important rule for taking the **very best care** of your rescue pup is...

to tell them

you love them.

More than owls love trees.

More than the whales love the sea.

And more than the stars love the moon.

Coming Soon!

HOW TO LOVE YOUR GOLDEN

FOLLOW US
on our social networks
@HOW2LOVEYOURPET

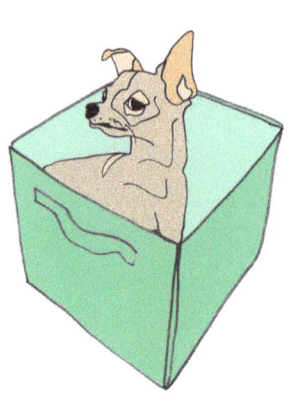

www.ingramcontent.com/pod-product-compliance
Lightning Source LLC
Chambersburg PA
CBHW061115070526
44583CB00027B/3308